THE BEST GOODBYE

Donna Wills RVN, PgCert A Phys, MIRVAP(VP)

Three dogs and a lamb publishing

Reviews

"Sobbing, brilliant, so much passion and compassion...
It will support so many caregivers.
He would be proud of you x"

Hannah Capon, Vet and Founder of CAM

"I've known Donna for many years and met Logan, so for me this book so resonates. It's so well written, its easy to read despite an emotional rollercoaster combining tears of sadness and joy being mixed into a heartfelt experience."

Anna Webb

"Donna Wills' book, 'The Best Goodbye,' deeply resonated with me. As a vet who specialises in home euthanasia services I've helped many families through this tough time and Wills' honest and tender writing reflects our shared commitment to making these final moments as peaceful as possible. This book is a must-read for anyone navigating pet loss."
☆☆☆☆☆
Dr Paul Manktelow

First Edition published 2024 by

Three Dogs and a Lamb Publishing
Bracknell, Berkshire. UK

Publisher Disclaimer: The events in this memoir are described according to the author's recollection; recognition and understanding of the events and individuals mentioned and are in no way intended to mislead or offend. As such the Publisher does not hold any responsibility for any inaccuracies or opinions expressed by the author. Every effort has been made to acknowledge and gain any permission from organisations and persons mentioned in this book. Any enquiries should be directed to the author.

All photographs copyright © of Donna Wills, except photos on P20 and P44, copyright © Brian Sidebotham
Cover image: Chrysa Grace / Dr Veronica Fowler
Printed in UK by IngramSpark

A CIP catalogue record for this book is available
from the British Library

ISBN 978-1-0687043-0-7

In loving memory of my dear Logan.

Forever in my heart.

Dedication

I dedicate this book to all those who have lost their best fur friends. I recognise that not everyone is able to control their goodbye and make it their best goodbye. My heart goes out to you all.

Contents

Acknowledgements

My husband and daughter for being the most wonderful support for Logan and I on this journey. We have loved and cared for him and each other. I also acknowledge my friends and family who have been a huge source of strength to us all. I am eternally grateful for all the love and hugs.

Donna Wills - Biography

I love animals and have spent my life working with them. They are my world, and I cannot imagine my life without them. Animals have always been by my side, so it was natural that I made them my career.

My earliest job was helping my uncle on his farm. My first paid work (after the obligatory paper round) was as a Kennel maid, and I loved it. My career path took me to veterinary nursing, where I then found a passion for rehabilitation. As a gymnast I was fascinated by the body's incredible response to healing using exercise. I wanted to see my patients thrive and that meant being more involved in their long-term care plans.

I established Animal Physiotherapy Ltd in 2005 and I love running my own company. I spend time making individual care plans for patients that work for their mums and dads too. Working for myself has led to so many amazing memories, like being the physio for the Pet Spa at Harrods, several TV appearances and lecturing to peers and vets. Most importantly it has allowed me to walk my own path in the veterinary industry, and help and support thousands of animals and caregivers from all over the world. I am immensely proud of that.

During this time, I have never lost my passion and love for both the patients and the "pet" parents. Being the care giver for an animal is a privilege, and I am honoured every time I am able to help. As a pet parent myself, I understand the emotional toll that worry for your loved one takes on the mind, body and soul.

My life journey has taught me so much about compassion and emotions. We get uncontrollably attached to our best friends, whether they are furry, scaly, feathery or bald and we all walk our own path with our emotions. When I realised my Logan was getting older, I feared his end. I had many years battling with my own pregrief, whilst supporting others with theirs. I then lost my boy and I had to cope with that indescribable pain. Nearly 2 years after losing my boy and still feeling swells of emotion, I realised it is highly unlikely that I am alone in my thoughts of loss and grief, so long after his passing. I felt a bubbling in my stomach that was only eased by writing. So I put pen to paper to get my thoughts down and that soon became this book.

Donna Wills RVN, PgCert A Phys, MIRVAP(VP)

Website: www.animalphysiotherapy.org.uk

Trigger Warning

Please be aware this book may evoke many emotions. It is designed to empower your thoughts before you say goodbye. However I do recognise that it may also evoke feelings of guilt and sadness over previous goodbyes. Life is a journey and we learn as we walk it. There is no judgment for choices we have made under the circumstances we are faced with. Warm hugs and strength to every reader for their own journey.

Preface

As I draw closer to the two-year anniversary of the passing of my boy, Logan, it still seems incredible how powerful and emotional my connection to him was and still is. I was driving home one night, reflecting on our years together after a Facebook memory popped up, showing him eating a birthday cake I had made him for his 15th birthday. I remember thinking, I didn't know he would get this far. I must make him a cake to celebrate. He loved that cake. I even made little carrot stick candles for it. 15 of them of course.

On this drive, I had an overwhelming feeling in my gut. I was missing my boy all over again. A tear came to my eye as I reflected on how hard I had worked to give him the best goodbye. I then felt I needed to share my story with the world to help others have their best goodbye as well.

My journey has taught me that I am not alone in my grief for my dog. Many people have shared their stories with me about how hard they too have found it. We are not alone.

At the end of the book, I have prepared a list of ideas that you may like to use to prepare for your goodbye. The true story I share here is how I worked through my journey to be able to collate this list.

Foreword

Hannah Capon, Vet and Founder of CAM

Atul Gawande, *Being Mortal: Medicine and What Matters in the End*

I am *privileged* to be a first opinion vet based in the UK. I say *privileged* because being entrusted to provide care for another's most precious possession comes with huge responsibilities, to both the caregiver and their companion, from the very beginning to the very end of their relationship. Throughout my years in practice I have supported many caregivers making the final arrangements for their beloved, and have witnessed the emotional anguish they endure in doing so. Having deeply empathetic, and considered resources, such as this book, to offer pet parents as they battle their inner conflicts are priceless tools.

I am also, and have been the privileged caregiver to my own beautiful souls, and as I read, the tears dripped uncontrollably from my chin. Donna's determination to ensure the last weeks with her beloved were as close to perfect as possible, triggered a tsunami of emotions. I too had suffered with anticipatory grief. Anxiety that didn't allow me the capacity to plan her passing. Instead even the briefest of thoughts of the event would consume me with guilt. A cruel paradox. I so desperately wanted Holly to pass in a manner that cemented my love for her, but my heart left my mind in tatters. I hope Donna's beautiful work gives carers the permission they need to honour their soul mates with a peaceful and heartfelt passing.

"Endings matter, not just for the person but, perhaps even more, for the ones left behind."

Atul Gawande, *Being Mortal: Medicine and What Matters in the End*

Logan

Logan was the most amazing dog in the whole wide world. I know everyone says that about their dog, but this is true. I also know everyone says that last part too! This is why I know how much everyone who is worth their salt loves their furbabies and wants them to be there, by their side forever.

Logan was my rock and my soul. He helped me through the most formative parts of my life. He stuck by me through thick and thin. There is no denying that you get true, unconditional love from your dog. It may also be true that you only get one "special one" in this world. Whether he was my one special boy in my lifetime or not, I don't know, all I know is how much he meant to me.

Before Logan

I had moved from the west country, where I lived with my parents and our family dog, Poppy. I loved all our dogs and all our other animals (I don't actually like the word pet, I struggle with it as it makes them seem like an object and I don't like that). I had connections with the local farmers and my uncle was also a farmer for a formative part of my youth.

When I arrived in Berkshire at my new job and new home, I was desperately lost and lonely. I understand this is normal. It was a whole heap of new. I was young, but I felt powerful and brave enough to make the move. However, I did drive home every weekend, back to my Poppy and my family and friends.

My new life grew, and I made new friends. I also got set up by the receptionist at the veterinary practice I worked at. She had eyes on me being a good daughter-in-law, so she sent her son into work with a tray of Christmas dinner, so that he would meet me. Clever lady! He liked me and soon after, rang me at work and asked me out. His mum was thrilled, and I was welcomed to the family.

I have a lot to thank this lady for as she also gave a big push to my career direction by encouraging me to enrol on a course and become an Animal Physiotherapist.

After a while, Pete and I bought a house together and that was it. I had made it to a settled life.

Poppy

By now I had also lost my Poppy dog. I loved that dog and it was an awful time. I was working as an emergency and critical care nurse when she got sick. The timing was incredible as I was also off sick having had four wisdom teeth removed in one sitting under full anaesthetic. As a result, I had been signed off work for a week, thank goodness.

I want to say this was my first experience of loss of a loved one. But it wasn't. Over the years I have had many animals in my life and therefore, also lost many. I lost Sooty, my Labrador, who my parents got when I was born so I never knew life without her until I was 16, when we heard a crash and she rolled off the bed, having an episode of some sort. I was young and not really aware of the details. All I know is that she was taken to the vets, and "helped along her way" or "put to sleep". Dad brought her back wrapped in a blanket and she was buried in the garden. I do remember I cried a lot but I didn't have much involvement in the process itself. My parents didn't prevent me from being involved, I was just too young to think about what I needed to do in that moment, and they were doing what they thought was best. I think they did well. I was not sheltered. She was brought home for us to bury and say our own goodbyes. I do now know, however, that it could have been a better goodbye.

After a short time, my friend told me her neighbour couldn't cope with their dog anymore, so she asked if we wanted her. My family has always been amazing animal lovers and keen rescuers. So that was a firm "yes" and along came Poppy.

She was also a family dog. I had a great connection with her. My family were always keen that no animal in our house belonged to anybody in particular. I think this was very healthy. No firm ownership and no one to blame for not taking responsibility of care or cost. We shared it all, though granted I didn't have to pay for her care as I was only a teenager at the time.

When I got the call from my mum to say Poppy was sick, I was desperately upset and worried. I was also supposed to be resting. However, the dog came first of course! My mum kept me updated. She looked like she may have somehow been poisoned on a walk. We certainly had no poison in the house; quite the opposite, in fact, we thought it was hilarious that we shared our cereal and clothing drawers with mice. Those free little spirits running around the house made us smile! I once woke up to find one climbing the TV aerial in my bedroom. It slipped and thumped onto the TV. It ran off so I assumed it was probably fine and I went back to sleep.

I rang the vets where I worked. We had emergency blood products in stock that would help if Poppy needed a blood transfusion. This was in the early days of blood transfusions, so whilst we knew how to do them, there was not a big list of dogs to call on for donations, and no blood banks. I drove into work, picked up the blood replacement bag and then drove to my parents' home, knowing it was there if needed. Many vets did not stock this life saving bag of expensive magic so we were fortunate.

By the time I arrived, the appointment was already made for the referral vets and we went off to Langford. Sadly, we were told Poppy had a liver tumour. A blood transfusion might give her a little more time, but she was now on her path to goodbye. She was brought back out to us happily riding on a trolley as she was weak, but alert, and we were given time to make a decision.

We opted not to let her suffer. She had treatment to relieve any pain and she was looking alert and happy, but we knew this was only temporary. My mum called our usual vets and booked her an appointment to euthanise her. There was some time to say goodbye. She could no longer manage the stairs or the steps to the back garden, so I took her into the front garden so she could enjoy some smells. I laid her on the bean bag that was her bed of choice. I joined her and we cuddled for about three hours. I cried a little but tried to enjoy the moment. We fed her some steak and then we took her to the vets for her goodbye. We were all with her and she knew we loved her dearly. She was cremated.

I know you may wonder why didn't we have the euthanasia done at home? The answer was, we were not wealthy. We had spent all our money on the veterinary care and the referral hospital. Home euthanasia was a cost we didn't have the money for. She was not really very stressed by the vets at this point, so we took comfort in that.

My biggest memory of coming home, the memory that still brings a twisted feeling in my gut, was trying to get back into the house. It was impossible. Every time I tried to go in the house, I couldn't stop the pain; the gut wrench followed by tears. I tried so hard. I just wanted to sit and rest as I was so tired, but I would see her bowls on the kitchen floor, and that was it, I was back out the door. It was too painful. I went down to the end of the back garden and sobbed, lying on her beanbag. My dad brought me out several cups of tea as he could see my pain. He also felt the pain and was dealing with it in his own way by making cups of tea for me. I even had to pee in the garden as I could not get back in that house.

As night came, it got cold and dark and I think I must have been all cried out, so I finally had to go in the house. More tears came, but I knew I had to be inside. I went to my room and started to try to heal my grieving.

I was a veterinary nurse. I had done courses on bereavement counselling. But none of that helps when you are in that moment yourself.

When I was ready, and somewhat pushed as my week of sick leave was at an end, I went back to my Berkshire home and continued to try to rebuild my life with no Poppy. As I had never lived there with her but only had her to stay when my parents were away, this was a little easier. But I knew there was no dog to come home to.

Logan's arrival

Now that my boyfriend and I had bought our house, there was room to get a furbaby. Animals are clearly my world. He knew that. I was actually very scared. As a vet nurse I know all the bad bits of having a furbaby. The sickness, and the cost which can be very scary. To add to that, I also knew the pain of the grief. That they do not last forever. I was very scared. But he was not.

I had worked for a time at the veterinary practice that looked after the residents of a local dog sanctuary. So that was the obvious place to go and see if we would find the furchild of our dreams. I had very firmly stated, "we will go and have a look, but no decisions will be made today". How foolish of me! We went to the sanctuary. They ran a very sensible policy of asking what you are thinking of and then bring out who they believe might fit the bill based on what you have told them.

I had asked for a border collie type as I just loved that breed type. She asked if I wanted all the beautiful feathers and fluff that comes with a collie. I answered, "no, it's not about looks, it's about personality I don't mind, so long as they think they are a collie". She also asked about age. I had said "around two years old". I wasn't foolish enough to want to deal with a puppy, and they find homes easier. I wanted an older dog.

She came out with Logan on a lead. He had been named Logan

Logan's first Christmas.
It was many years ago...

by the home, based solely on what letter they had come to for that day's intake. I did think it was a great name! We took Logan for a walk to get to know him. He was far younger than I had suggested, probably only five or six months and he had clearly not been loved. He had cuts on his hind paw pads. It was so sad, but despite all this, he was a very happy boy. I really only cared that I could touch him all over and do any examination necessary. He allowed all this despite me being new to him.

Well, that was that. So much for having a look and then taking time to decide. It was love at first sight and I have now learnt I am incapable of leaving a stray behind, so I must make all decisions before I attempt to visit a rescue centre.

We both wanted him. I remained scared as that's what happens when you know too much. We drove straight from the rescue centre, to the vets so we could pick up the four weeks instant free pet insurance and get him registered and that was that. We now had our boy firmly in our lives and in our arms.

Logan and I

My bond with Logan did nothing but grow and grow over the days, months and years. By now I had started my post graduate certificate in Animal Physiotherapy and he was my daily guinea pig! He also helped me study. Once I qualified, he helped me build my business. He was the face of the company, a demo dog for lectures, an inspiration for blogs and ideas, an anecdote and story to tell clients for motivation. He was, quite simply, a super star.

When I became the animal physiotherapist for the Pet Spa at Harrods, Logan's life took a super cool twist. Now he was coming into London with me. The big smoke. The scary concrete jungle. As a former country bumpkin, I was pretty scared of London and had been repeatedly reduced to tears by its intimidating size, sounds and smells. All the stories us country folk are told about what goes on in the big smoke did not help. In the back of your mind, you are convinced your bag needs to be as secure as the bank of England, you must never go down any quiet roads otherwise you will be stabbed and never cross a road as you will be run over. As a child I actually believed children did not live in London. We were only allowed to visit because it was way too dangerous to actually live there. I know that is crazy now, but I honestly thought it for many of my young years.

Don't get me wrong. By now I had been into London several

times and I had discovered that my childhood beliefs about London were completely wrong, however, I did still find it a bit scary and overwhelming. As a result, I was incredibly glad that my boy was allowed to come in with me on so many occasions. I was ridiculously proud to take my boy into Harrods, a very posh and high-end department store. He was working with me and some amazing privileges came with that. I always put a high visibility coat on him as I didn't want him to get hurt. This meant that when we got on the train (he loved the train) people often moved and insisted I sat down with him, despite me explaining that I was fine, and the coat was simply for his protection. One man even offered him a drink of water out of his own hand. It was an amazing opportunity to see the

Logan in his working life, helping me. We did a demonstration of massage for Crufts extra. Clare Balding and Allan Carr were the kindest people and Logan loved the giant sausage Clare gave him after the show!

lovely side of Londoners.

I must share that at Harrods, there were a tremendous number of media moments. Logan became very famous for being "that doggy in the window". The spa had a day where we were working in one of Harrods windows as a display. This was huge. It's very expensive and prestigious to work in a window of Harrods. We were there all day. Frankly, he could not have been happier. Hours of lying and being massaged by his mummy. For me, hours of sitting massaging and loving my boy. We were a team. There must have been thousands of photos taken of us that day alone.

As anyone can testify, relationships with humans are complicated and difficult at times. My boyfriend and I split up. I was now a single fur child mum. Pete continued to pay the pet insurance, and I did appreciate that, but the care was down to me.

During that break up there were many, many tears, and Logan would come and snuggle into my neck when I was sad. Oddly we seemed to develop our own language. I would make a little "humm" sound and he would come and jump up on the bed behind me and put his head over my neck for a cuddle every time. It was so cute and exactly what I needed.

As his soul mummy, I had to take him everywhere when it would be too long to leave him at home alone. This meant at times he would come to work with me. Luckily in my profession that wasn't impossible. But it also wasn't ideal. So, there were many occasions I would have to drive home every lunch time to make sure he was let out and all was well.

Logan had shown many quirks over the years. When young he was super cheeky. If he got out of the house and didn't want to come in, he would have a tantrum. This meant rolling on his back and sticking his long front legs up in the air. Then, when I went to grab him or his collar, he would stick his paws into my body and chest and push me away. He was just the right size to mean I couldn't grab him at all! It really made us all laugh.

He was incredible with other animals too. If he saw a cat, he might consider being a brave dog and chasing the cat, but often the cat wouldn't move and if he got even slightly close, he would do a wide circle around it and slowly come back a little embarrassed that he didn't catch it, nor make it even care enough to move. Once and once only, he caught a squirrel. We were all shocked as he was never that fast, but he instantly stopped and spat it out. It ran up the tree and he stared at me as if to say "ooops! Yikes! Not doing that again!" He hadn't been bitten by the squirrel, but it was clearly not really in his nature as he never did it again.

After I split up from Pete, I needed a new house mate. I couldn't afford my home and therefore, my mortgage, on my own. My friend came to the rescue. She moved in and bought the house with me. Now she also had to love my boy too. This was easy. He was very lovable!

The stories continued. Carolyn loved a bath. Logan used to come in the bathroom when I had a bath as he liked eating the bubbles that popped up over the side of the bathtub. I didn't mind, it made me laugh. When Carolyn wanted a bath, she would often ask "Donna, are you sure he won't get in my bath?" He often looked inquisitive, and he was cheeky and used to love to drink the bath water but I confidently said "no, he won't actually get in." Until one day I got a message on my phone "Donna, he got in my bath!" I can't lie, I wailed with laughter. I genuinely didn't see that coming. Thankfully, Carolyn also laughed a lot too.

I came home once to find the fridge door open. I looked at Logan and he looked at me with a guilty look in his eye then he turned slightly and I saw something stuck to his front leg. It then swung around the front of his leg. The cheeky monkey had eaten a pack of prawns! The only evidence left was the packaging stuck to his leg. How could I not laugh. Poor boy couldn't hide the evidence away, it was literally stuck to him. I am sure he enjoyed the prawns though!

There were also more serious bonding moments. He had health problems. Of course, he did, he belonged to a nurse. He had idiopathic haematuria for about a year. This meant he would go flying down the stairs, desperate to go out to urinate, and not always making it in time. I would also find blood in his wee. He had lots of investigation and medication and nothing worked to resolve it, that is until the threat of the referral service. For some completely unknown reason, as quickly as it came, it went. That is the joy of the idiopathic disease, the name we give to any ailment when we just don't really know why it's going on. I concluded all he really needed was three thousand pounds worth of investigation and that seemed to work!

I also had to resolve his poor paws. As I mentioned earlier, when I adopted him, his paws were split open. It was only his back paws and it was symmetrical damage on both sides. It looked rather suspiciously like they had been cut open on purpose as they were deep cuts. I wanted him to start agility as I thought that would be good for his mind, but I couldn't risk making his paws worse. They needed daily care, cleaning and moisturising and a walk regime that would not make them worse.

He didn't mind at all as this led to even more one on one mummy time. I did trick training with him instead. He was so clever! He learnt his left and right and would shake the correct paw you asked for. He could tell me secrets. I would hold my hand to my ear and ask him "tell mummy a secret, whisper" and he would do a quiet "woof!" Occasionally he might shout a loud bark. I would say, "don't shout, whisper" and he would do his little quiet "woof". It was so cute! I taught him to waltz, present, put a ball in the bowl and so much more! Put a ball in the bowl was hilarious. From that point on you could never leave a bowl on the floor as you would always come back to find a ball in it! One of my favourites was "teach mummy how to join the SAS" he would then crawl on his belly along the floor.

Logan was there for more make ups and break ups, as I sadly had a longer string of wrong boyfriends than I care to admit to. Logan welcomed all of them with kindness. Perhaps more kindness for some than others. He was a great judge of character and likely, better than me. But I was still growing up and he was my sidekick, there to pick me up and dust me off as needed.

Logan and the family

Eventually, I found the right man, and Logan was right there. Brian had never had a dog before. But thankfully and rightly so, (otherwise he would not have been the right man) he took Logan on as his fur baby too. I am so proud to be able to say that he loved him and cared for him for all the rest of his days, equally as much as I did.

At our wedding, Logan was the ring bearer. Brian accepted completely that this was an essential part of the wedding day, and no venue was acceptable unless it was going to support that completely! This ruled out the whole of Surrey, but that was fine, we still had Berkshire. We finally found our venue. Logan had a vest made and he even had a bow tie the same as the best man and groom. The best man knew the importance of Logan's role and did him justice. Logan even had my friend as his plus one. This made us all so happy. My bridesmaids led him down the aisle, or maybe he led them. After the ceremony, he bit at the bubbles we had instead of confetti. It was so beautiful. He was, of course, part of our wedding photos. The chef even gave him his own wedding breakfast. I was blessed to have my boy with us. It was desperately sad that we had to leave him behind for the honeymoon, but he was in good hands.

The next momentous occasion in our lives was bringing our skin child home from the hospital. Childbearing was not an easy task for me. I had endless problems. I had to finish work earlier than I hoped as I was having trouble. I had my beautiful baby girl and eventually was allowed home. Brian had been in care overdrive. He had the boy, and I had the girl whilst we were trapped in the hospital. I was glad to get home, but once home I had to recuperate. I was blessed to have so many friends who could help me. My mum came as often as she could but lived an hour away and she was still working. My friend, who had been Logan's plus one at the wedding, stepped up and came to take my boy out for his walk every day for about three months, which was so kind of her. She would even let herself in the house and pick him up quietly if I was asleep. All new mums have to sleep when they can, especially us poorly ones.

Logan took to being a big brother so well! He preferred that Paige didn't actually touch him, but he took on the caring protector role with full force. One time she was crying and I had done everything I could think of, changed her nappy, fed her, cuddled her, but she was overtired. I just didn't know what to do. So, I put her on her on her sensory blanket and walked away to get a moment to think about what might be up. Logan, who often was by my side when she cried, stayed next to her. Next thing I know, he is stamping on the floor with his paw! I looked at him and he points his nose to Paige and stamps again. It was almost like her was saying "come on, you got this, don't ignore her". I picked her up and carried on with the cuddling and she eventually fell asleep. But in that moment, he was the added strength I needed. I thank him for that as he was so often my strength and my rock.

As Paige grew, their bond also grew. Paige used to stroke his ear whilst sucking her finger. She called it "softing". He was never far from either of our sides. In fact, he disliked any of us not being in the same room together. This was probably the collie in him. If someone was upstairs and someone down, he would often run between the two, starring at you and pointing to the other person suggesting that you all be in one place together.

Logan grew and evolved through his long life, but one thing is clear, he left a stream of strong memories for us to hold dearly forever. To this day, Paige writes stories about him, and he remains in her mind. I am so proud that this is the case.

His grey years

Logan and I at the beach

As nature intended, Logan aged. At twelve years old I knew this to be around typical "life expectancy". At this point I became painfully aware of his mortality. I didn't want to be aware of this, but I was. Nothing I could do would stop me thinking about the fact that he was now on borrowed time. I knew this was what we call "pre-grieving". Grieving before the event has even occurred. It's really silly and sounds very foolish on paper. What is the point in the added emotion of worrying about something that hasn't happened. What does that solve? Nothing. But yet, no matter how much I knew this was silly, it was there anyway. Maybe it was a defence mechanism. My brain trying to prepare me somehow for what was coming. The stark reality is, there is no preparing. It is just pointless as you will not reduce the goodbye pain at all. I wish I could take away pre-grief. But that said, I think it is what allowed me to do all the things that followed, that helped me give him the best goodbye.

As he started to age, because I was an animal physio I was completely aware of his needs. As he started to struggle in any areas, I adapted his care plan accordingly. In the early stages this meant changes to his walk plan, more massages, and some muscle building exercises. Over time he started to have further needs and so some low-level medication was started.

No two old age care plans are the same, and nor should they be. There are no two dogs with the same bodies and lives. Every plan is always only right for that individual. I did my research and I worked out my plan. It evolved as he needed it to. I looked into things like stem cell therapy, but they just didn't seem right for him. I was pleased I had done the research and made the right choice for him and us.

During this time, he continued to be happy. Each year that went by shocked me. His thirteenth birthday, wow, I was amazed, he was so active and happy. His fourteenth Birthday, wow, I was amazed, he was still so active and happy. His fifteenth Birthday, wow, I was amazed, he was so active and happy. I must admit, at fifteen years old, I had thought we would not see another birthday. Imagine my joy when he made it to his sixteenth birthday! I do always tell people, don't try to plan for reaching a set birthday. That can blur your vision when truly looking at your dog's heart and whether he or she is happy. I stand by that, and I don't ever look for a goal to reach, but I was still thrilled when he did reach the milestones. At sixteen we knew that would be his last year but we treated each day as it came.

At about fourteen years old, something changed in him. It had clearly been coming on slowly over the past year or two, but when something changes so slowly, it's hard to recognise it. At that point we entered the phase of what is called in the human world "the night crazies". In dogs this is to do with canine cognitive dysfunction. In humans, we call this dementia. It hit us hard when he entered the phase of waking up at around midnight every night, and pacing. It took time for us to work out that it was not that he needed to go out to the toilet (which is what we thought at first), but he wanted to take back control. It was from talking to human dementia care staff that I was able to learn about all the human symptoms, and realised they are so similar. I did lots of research and we made many changes, changed his diet, added supplements, gave him more mental stimulation, and lick mats to appease his repetitive behaviour needs (he loved to lick cold things like the glass patio doors or the sink pedestal). I am so proud to say that after six weeks of Brian and I tag teaming sleeping on the sofa so that Logan could be downstairs (as this is where he wanted to be when the night crazies hit), the phase passed. In human terms, he may not have known who the prime minister was, but he was Logan again, and a very happy Logan who loved his cuddles and wanted to sleep through the night again, up in our room as he always had. In case this moment has sparked the question "why didn't they just leave him downstairs to sleep if he wanted to be downstairs", well, Logan didn't want to be upstairs, but he also didn't want to be alone downstairs, so when we took him down, if we went up, he would bark. We had to learn what his ever-changing needs were. Six weeks felt like forever at the time, but in hindsight, it was nothing and well worth the effort.

I felt that professionally he had been a big part of my career success for all the time I had my business. This was for so many reasons, but now it was because I was the carer of an aging dog. I was old enough to understand the full implications of what he was experiencing. Due to my work, I was in a privileged position to be able to know what to do. As a result, he was frequently the inspiration for many blogs and informative videos on caring for the geriatric and osteoarthritic patient.

I was also super proud of my family. My daughter had learnt that his aging needs were of huge importance, and she would have to learn love and patience. My husband had to learn to care in the way I did. He took that on board with full gusto. This meant clearing up after accidents and lifting him up and down the stairs on his command.

When stairs become too much, he was fabulous at recognising it. He would bark so you came to help him with both up and down. After about a year of carrying him up and down the stairs I said to Brian, "this is crazy and dangerous, we need to find a better solution". I looked into stair lifts. I was sad to see there were no dog stair lifts. I was even more mortified when I did come across one company who claimed to sell "dog stair lifts". I rang them to ask for a photo. They said, there is no photo as it looks the same as a human stair lift. Confused, I asked how that worked. She replied, that you get them to sit on the seat. I was horrified. Ok, so maybe you can get a little

Yorkshire Terrier to sit on the seat, but that is not safe or secure, how do they not fall off? The answer I got was that they can sell me a harness! I was outraged at the thought of the dog now hanging by a harness over the edge of a seat not actually designed for his safety. More importantly to me, this was not going to be the answer for a Border Collie!

I took to YouTube. Surely, I can't be the first person with this problem to solve. I found a few on there that were inspiring, but all had their complexity. In the end, Brian took over the job of solving the problem. We managed to find a human stair lift, for free on Facebook Marketplace. Brian had the skill to be able to adapt it and make a box to go on it so my boy would be safe in his stair journey. I was thrilled. I decorated the box as a VW campervan with the number plate WOOF 1. Logan took to this so well. He loved it and felt safe. He always trusted us for all we did, but you could tell when you were pushing his trust boundaries. Thank you, Brian, for the huge effort in installing a stair lift into our home. It remains there to this day, for any future dogs that may need this safety feature.

There were other adaptions for the family. He became more incontinent over time. It became a funny running joke. He would have a specific tail angle when he was about to poop. Anyone in the family might be the first to see it and in fact, that was often Paige, our daughter. She would shout "poo tail, poo tail" and we would all come running, one would grab the tissue to pop under him and get him cleaned up, and the other would grab any other cleaning equipment needed to sort everything. In the end we were sensible enough to keep washable incontinence sheets under his bum for those moments. But he really didn't mind and neither did we. He could get up off the floor, the trouble was, when he tried, the extra effort often made him poop inadvertently, bless him.

As time went on, we got more mobility aids and tried more therapies. He had a bash at hydrotherapy. It was good but he became a snappy crocodile in the pool. He had his special therapist who knew him well and was happy to swim him despite his crocodile face. He didn't like being turned around in the pool, bless him. After his ten sessions we left that one to continue the therapies that made him smile. His therapist became his friend as well though. When he got sick a few months later, she visited as I had him at home. There was no way I as a vet nurse, was not going to have him home and under my care. She dropped him round her home-made bone broth, which was so kind of her, particularly as she left quite a lot of the chicken in it! He found his crocodile face again, just for her. As naughty as that was, it was also a good sign he was getting better!

We were exhausted as we (both Brian and I) had been sleeping next to him all night and giving him critical care and love. We were desperately scared at this stage as he had pneumonia and he needed intravenous fluids. As a nurse I could look after all this safely. I had done so for many years at work, and veterinary care has changed greatly over twenty years. We didn't have many drip pumps when I started, so I was very able to work in a home environment, and he was very grateful to be at home. I think district nursing is something that should be massively encouraged in the veterinary world. There are already some amazing veterinary district nurses, but very few. We slept by his side and made a wall with our bodies, assuming we would wake up if he moved as he would have to step over us. One morning, after three days of illness, to our amazement and happiness, he was clearly feeling better as he had stepped over us and we found him lying the other side of us. We woke up to see him staring at us as if to say, "what is all this then, what's all the fuss?". I always felt as though I knew exactly what he was saying. He had pulled through just fine in the end.

I decided to get a cargo bike. This meant I could now pop the dogs into the cargo bike to get them to places to walk without the long walk to get there in the first place. By now we also had Swagger, a three-legged boy, who Logan chose to welcome with open arms. Swagger came into my life through work and desperately needed a new mum as his dad didn't want him anymore due to him being injured. It was desperately sad, but I said we could only have him if Logan accepted him. When they met, they just got on so well, and Logan took him under his wing and looked after him. He also had needs that needed comforting mentally. Logan had the biggest heart.

In time, the cargo bike was not enough. We needed something that we could use to take Logan with us when we went out as a family, so we didn't have to leave him at home. We had cameras in the house to watch him and we could race back if he had done anything silly and needed help, but we didn't want to keep leaving him behind due to us having to do family things that required several hours of walking, so we got a buggy. I was worried that he wouldn't take to it and it certainly wasn't cheap, but it turned out to be the best purchase we ever made. He took to it so well and we now had freedom again.

It's worth sharing some of the funny stories with the buggy. It took a little time to get him to stay lying down in it. There were some moments he fell over as he stood and then I stopped to make him lie down and then he fell because I stopped, so that took time to work out. He then learned to do a little low bark to ask to get out, which was great. I used the buggy to get him to the park, or anywhere else. He would get out for a wander and then, when he was tired, I popped

Logan in buggy on a family walk, pushed by my husband

him back in the buggy. There were many times when he wanted to get out because he saw other dogs. Whether this was due to street cred, or just wanting to interact in some way, we will never know, but he made those choices and I was proud to be able to let him. That buggy gave him a few years of happiness and us too as there was now more freedom. We took him out when we wanted to see the Christmas lights. We didn't have to worry. We wrapped him up in blankets so he was not going to get cold and off we went. Swagger was able to fit in too, although he was young, he had only three legs, so this was helpful for him too. We could also take him to special places, like the beach. The beach was a hard trip without it. He truly loved the beach, but the loud wind mixed with his failing hearing meant he would wander off after anyone who looked like two adults and a child so the buggy was so much safer for him. It was impressive the speed he had on his super-fast amble after a chosen target. Particularly when we were also trying to watch another dog and a young child.

My biggest worry

Remember through all of this I was pre-grieving. This meant I felt like I always needed a plan for the goodbye. This was the only way I felt I could be in control in some way and feel like it was all somehow going to be ok, even though I knew I was going to lose my best friend at any point.

Maybe it was the fact that I had also been a vet nurse for so many years, and seen so many goodbyes, that I knew mostly what I didn't want. I feared my boy feeling any sort of stress. I knew I would be a mess. That was a given and a total side note to the problem, but I did not want my boy stressed and worried. I think it's fair to say we all fear the unknown.

I do want to add that I am very proud of my years as a nurse. I know I wanted a totally perfect goodbye for my boy, but I am proud to say that every goodbye I was a part of was a peaceful one. We always respected and supported the mums and dads at their hardest moments. We gave hugs if it seemed appropriate, we gave them time, we explained everything. But at the end of the day, we didn't know what that mum and dad's perfect goodbye actually was in their heads. They didn't work in the profession so it was likely they had no idea what really was to come and it was far easier to dismiss it in their heads.

When I was an emergency nurse, I think that was the hardest part of the job. Remember I have been in the profession for over twenty years. I worked in it when mums and dads saw the regular family vet and formed bonds with them. As an emergency nurse we didn't know any of these pet parents. We just had to be kind and caring to them all, but we had never known their loved one before that day or night. Even more sadly, nobody goes to the emergency vet for their expected and planned goodbye. If they know it's coming and have had time to say goodbye, it's done with their favourite vet at their favourite practice, or even better, at home.

Covid came when my boy was aging, and this caused a huge pang of worry. Now I was faced with the most awful dilemma of all, would my boy even be with me when I had to say goodbye. I couldn't handle the thought of not being there for him. I was desperately reading the posts on the veterinary forums, where vets and nurses reach out and ask questions. There were endless discussions about euthanasia, and how we could do it in a covid safe fashion. The vets were so keen to make it a priority to do the best they could. They turned to doing it outside and placing long lines in the loved one's limbs so that they could then give the beloved back to the mum or dad to cuddle and they could go to sleep in their arms. But home visits were now a big no no. We can't ignore that there were also the sad, sad few who had an awful, lonely goodbye, whilst the poor vets tried to figure out a new way. The vets didn't want this. They loved these fur babies. This is why they entered the profession in the first place. Up and down the country there was story after story of disgusting emotionally cruel, dark, barbaric behaviours, all in the name of Covid. Funerals that loved ones couldn't attend, elderly people dying on their own with no one allowed to hold their hand, other than the care staff who happened to be on shift. With that in the news and in my mind, how could I expect special treatment for my boy? I was so desperate, that I was even thinking about how I can convince the vet to just hand me the syringe, so that I could do it myself, but I really didn't want that responsibility. I was actually impressively good at placing cannulas in veins with tears in my eyes. I had discovered this during my working life. I didn't want this now, but I was never going to be away from my boy for his goodbye. It was not going to happen but how could I convince a vet to allow me to do this? What vet knew I had this skill? I hadn't done it in years. It was not a perfect goodbye. But these thoughts ran through my mind daily and it fuelled my biggest fear.

How will he go? How will I say my goodbye? What is perfect for our family and my boy?

I knew what I wanted. At home, in his happy place. Privacy to set it how it should be. This was my perfect and his perfect goodbye.

I was scared. I remained scared for years. What if it happens at night? What if it's an emergency and I have to take him to the emergency vets? I could just about handle taking him to our normal day vets, but it was definitely less than ideal and not what I or we, wanted.

I set about finding options. Now my head was buzzing with ideas for a business to help other people like me in this dilemma. I knew it was a big problem and I was not alone. The more I spoke to people the more I realised that many other people felt as I did.

Thankfully, as time passed, Covid did too. Rules were relaxed and I could let my worry disperse slightly. But actually, the problem had just evolved and changed. Now the vets were so busy catching up on all the non-emergency patients whose treatment or appointments had been delayed because of Covid. Now there was no time for home visits. For me, cost was not an issue. That boy had dedicated his whole life to loving me and I would give him the world back. I didn't care about cost and my husband fully supported this. But it was very clear that prices were going up and home visits would be expensive. I just had to suck it up; at least it was now looking more possible.

This didn't solve the problem of an out of hours emergency. I still was terrified of a sudden decline that might mean it was time to say goodbye during the night. I had to find a better plan.

My Team

I am very much a believer in a team approach to everything. I do not believe in putting all your eggs in one basket. Some might say there is a lack of loyalty in this approach, but I think it's self-preservation and a way of improving your chances of the best outcome. I started to reach out.

I had a friend who, last time we spoke, was still a nurse at the emergency vet service, so I checked in with her. I hoped that if that had to happen, maybe I'll be lucky and it would be her on that night. We shall see.

I reached out to other vets including a friend I worked with many years ago. She now had a mobile veterinary service. She set it up because she cared and I was so grateful to her. She said, just try her. I didn't expect her to be on call 24/7 for me, but I did trust that if she saw my call and happened to be up and able, she would come. I was out of her area, and she knew this, but I knew she would come. This was some relief as maybe I would be able to have a little more daytime cover to take me into the evening, and she provided home visits so this was helpful. I knew she would care as well as she is lovely and when we worked at our old practice together, they actually had a farewell room, especially dedicated to the goodbye, so she understood.

I still needed more though. I plucked up the courage to ask my usual practice what their current protocol was for home visits and euthanasia. I was scared to ask because I was worried they might tell me they couldn't fit them in anymore due to being busy. They were a lovely practice, so I didn't want to believe this would be true, but it was a worry, so for a while, I did that very foolish thing of sticking my head in the sand and hoping it would all be rosy. Eventually I asked the question, and I am glad I did. They were amazing. They still did home visits and they said to try to give as much notice as possible but they would do their best. I can't deny, of course the first thought was "notice, how will I ever be able to give notice?" and "do their best", I really wanted a firm, yes we will be there no matter what! But this was unrealistic. Yes, it's what I needed and wanted but deep down I knew it was not realistic. You can tell how unrealistic it was by seeing my fear of even asking about all of these things. But it is fair to say that practice, and all their vets, have never let me down. They had always been super sympathetic to me and my needs and always done their best by me and my boy. But this was the biggest moment so it was a worry.

It's funny in reflection. I consider the goodbye to be the biggest moment, the one that has to be so perfect. Yet on the occasions where he fell ill, at no point did I worry about that in the same way. Of course, he had to pull through and I was desperately worried about him being ill, but I never felt the need to plan for his illnesses in this way. His goodbye is the most final act. The one where he doesn't come back and the outcome is the same every time if you think of it clinically. Disease is what you recover from and you remember all the trauma you might experience during it, yet that was never my biggest worry. As a nurse, maybe I felt a bit more in control of this bit because I would have my boy back, I knew a lot about his care and I knew if I needed to question the choices being made. I was also lucky enough to feel like I was an asset to the care team for my boy during his illnesses. The vets made me part of the care team and we made decisions together. But his goodbye, that had to be exactly how I wanted it, all on my terms. Selfishly I felt strongly that the perfect goodbye was the only option, no matter how much pressure and stress that put on my shoulders.

I also want to share that I reached out to pretty much all the vets I knew in my area, who might be able to help. I was preparing myself and them that I might phone them. They all knew me and my connection with my boy. I am very proud of my industry and proud to report that not one rejected my plea and all said to let them know when the time came and they would see what they could do. I did feel empowered but I was still worried about the night time hours.

I eventually turned to the dreaded internet. The place where you can find amazing things, but also dreadful things. I was looking to see if there were any other places that might offer home visits. I actually found a few companies and my heart missed a beat! Wow! How did I not know there were euthanasia services available that specifically do home visits!

I looked through the websites and contacted only one. It was the only one that covered my area. I crossed my fingers and awaited my reply. I am so sad to report that I had no reply and my heart sank. After a few days I thought I would follow it up. We all know emails can go to spam, after all. Finally I did get a reply. But it didn't make any sense and wasn't particularly warm. Maybe I had unrealistic expectations. I wanted to be wrapped in a duvet and hugged so tight that I felt it would all be perfect and now was not the time to worry anymore. But that didn't happen. The other vets I had contacted had been amazing and clearly nothing could now match that. On further reading of the website it looked like the service still only actually worked from 8am until 8pm anyway, so I decided to park it and not chase it. It was not the energy I needed in my life for this situation. I was starting to feel as organised as I possibly could be.

Whilst all this level of organising did not make the worry go away completely, it did ease my soul as much as was possible.

It was time

It is quite incredible how emotional it is to write about this even though my boy has been gone nearly two years. This just proves how hard it is on our soul. I am ok with this though, as it just makes me warm inside, that I loved my boy so much, I would do anything for him and it was true love as he still resides firmly in my heart to this day, and will forever. We still say good night to his urn and ashes on occasion.

Deciding it was time was the hardest thing I have ever had to do. This was my boy. Not the family fur baby. My parents couldn't step in and make the decision now. Of course, my husband was part of the family and he helped. He made it very clear that he would never go against my thoughts and so it really was all on my shoulders. But in all honesty, had he disagreed with me, I doubt I would have listened.

As it became more evident that Logan's mobility was deteriorating and his incontinence was getting worse, we talked more and more about his health. We reflected frequently on his quality of life. We actually felt incredibly lucky and privileged that we could both be home all the time with him as we both worked from home. The single blessing that came from Covid, was that now my husband was also home to help with Logan's growing care needs.

My mum works in elderly human care. We often talked about quality of life and diseases of the elderly. It was actually fascinating to compare, and I often reflected on how much is missed on both the human and animal side. Never the same things on both sides oddly. Humans need much more physio care than they get offered. Animals need way more constipation care, amongst many other things, that are just not recognised. It was very interesting.

Logan had got to the stage where his walking was more difficult. But it was clear he was still happy, very happy in fact, as he lived for cuddles. He still went out on his walks every day. I had actually found quite a comfort in blogging and vlogging the care levels he was getting on a daily basis as I knew I was sharing the possibilities with others who may not be aware of them. He had the buggy to get to his walks which gave him so much joy. On the stroll he would get out and walk if he wanted to, but by now he was not so able to balance. I got him a sling to try to help but he was so cheeky, that he just sat in it and said "fine, you carry my butt then", so that didn't work for us. But it was fine, he was very happy to walk with his mummy as a walking stick. I held him for walks with my hand between his back legs. I didn't actually need to lift him, just support his balance so he didn't fall over. He could then do all the walking and sniffing that he wanted. Yes, it was back breaking but I didn't care. Thankfully my husband and I shared the work.

We had some beautiful last walks. There were several whilst we observed and decided. It was such a slow decline that we did have time. In the end he was not so keen to walk forwards either and that was the moment we said those dreaded words "I think it's time" and followed it with tears.

Logan was still super happy. When you stood him up his little perky face shone and his ears were still up high, so I felt no guilt in delaying it by enough days to get all the pieces of the puzzle in place.

His incontinence was also getting worse. We were more than happy to clean him up as much as was needed, but I was aware that the clean-up was not completely fun for him. There is always a risk that he might get urine scalding and sore skin from lying in his own urine. Of course, we cleaned him up every morning and it was really only where he had urinated over-night, that he was wet. But we felt guilty. As with the mobility, he was not going to get sores over the space of a week. We were just aware that it was another reason why it was time to say goodbye.

I painfully rang the vets on the Tuesday and asked if they could come out on the Friday, after school so that our daughter could also be there. They agreed without any hesitation. It was booked. I did always have to have the caveat that I could cancel if anything changed and that was of course fine with the vets.

It was so hard to know what to do for the best with our daughter, Paige. She was only seven years young at the time. We knew it would be very hard for her to process, but children all handle these things differently. We had been preparing her by talking about him dying and she understood this was the normal cycle of life. She didn't want it to happen anymore than we did, but she had to know what our plans were. We will never know if we handled things "correctly" or not, but we do know that Paige is totally fine. She talks about him to this day, and we allowed her to make her own choices of what she wanted to do for each step of the journey.

We did decide not to tell her until the Thursday before, as we didn't want her worrying about it, but we did want her to have time to think about any questions she might have. We also told her school teachers so that they knew, were able to support her, and call us if we needed to collect her from school. She took it very well. She still wanted to go to school on the Friday before it all happened, and we felt strongly that she should do what she wanted as this was also her journey and path to walk her way.

After I had called the vets to book the home visit, I felt some relief as I finally knew it would be at home. I felt hugely upset knowing I had booked my boy's goodbye, but I felt proud that we had looked after him so well and were now giving him the dignified goodbye I had always wanted for him. I still felt scared that he might not make it to the Friday. Waiting was the right thing though. Sometimes dogs perk up again and find a second wind. I felt I had to give him that chance. I didn't want to be that mum that waits too long but I had to give him his chance, just in case. It is fair to say I was conflicted. My husband agreed with it all and felt all the same conflicting emotions.

I knew that I wanted him cremated. I also knew that every one of my vets used a fairly local cremation service, Dignity in Hook, that everyone thought very highly of. As a result, this was going to be the only place that would touch my boy once he had gone. I still wanted full control. I looked on their website to see how to contact them. I decided to take a look around the website. I'm not even sure why, since as a nurse, I had dealt with them so often, I felt like I knew their "menu" inside and out.

To my surprise, and delight, I saw they did an attended cremation service. I was intrigued and looked further at this. I had already decided in my mind that we were going to drive Logan there ourselves and make sure he was treated with the utmost dignity for as long as possible. Now I see there is no reason I can't see him right until his shell is laid to rest. I knew his spirit would be with me. I knew this was only his earthly transport vessel, but I wanted to make sure it still had the dignified goodbye it deserved. I rang the crematorium and spoke to the mostly lovely lady on the phone, who was so understanding. She booked him in for his attended service at 11am on the Saturday. So perfect. No rushing. No prolonged waiting around. Just enough time to say a respectful goodbye and look after him for that last part of his journey. I was actually so happy to have this in place. I finished the call with "and it's ok if I change my mind and have to postpone this isn't it?" She replied, "yes of course". I was in a little cloud of organised bliss. It was a strange feeling, I had been so worried for so many years, that knowing it was all finally going according to plan was a huge weight off my shoulders.

All that was left was to make the best of his last few days. We certainly did this. There were many, many tears, but we did this.

There was another issue to work around. Children are unpredictable and I had no idea how my daughter was going to be with all this. It's easy to think she will be devastated and will handle it like any adult. But I knew that when I was much younger, my perspective of death was not like it is now. I had lost lots of hamsters with very little upset after the event. I was upset, but not crying and like I felt about it now. I felt I didn't want to make plans on her behalf. On that Friday, there was a party she was due to go to with her friends. Despite losing Logan on Friday, maybe being around her friends would be just what she needed. On the other hand, maybe it will be horrible, and she will be a blubbering mess and ruin the party. We decided to expand the care team again. I called another friend who I knew I could trust to help. She also had to take her son to the same party. I explained the whole thing. We knew there was no chance we would be taking her to this party, so, it was decided that our friend will swing by on the way to the party. If Paige wants to go, she can go, if she wants to stay, she can stay and if she gets to the party and is upset, it's very close by and our friend would turn around and bring her straight home. This was a tall request of our friend, but she was a star. She both agreed and supported the whole idea. I contacted the mum of the party so that she also knew the game plan and understood that if there were any issues then Paige would be whisked out. The mum also agreed it was a good plan. I felt so supported and this really helped.

His last few days

Now all the official plans were in place there was nothing more formal that needed to be done. Now we could just love him. We took to this with all our heart and soul. I still had to work, as did Brian, but we tag teamed for all his needs.

Our last walk at Heathlake. He enjoyed the January sun whilst looking over the lake

We just sat with him and had a chat by the lake. Such peace.

Swagger joined us on our last walk and looked over
the lake peacefully too.

It was very hard work. My husband was working in IT so only had to deal with himself to a larger extent. This was helpful at this emotional time. I had to be with my clients and patients which I found very hard. I frequently held back the tears. Many of my clients, are really friends, so I shared my journey and felt so much support and love. It was so touching. My world was finally the squishy duvet I had needed for all these years.

Wednesday

On the Wednesday, Brian and I took the boys out to Heathlake. We took Logan's bed as we knew this was our final walk at this spot. He loved this place to walk. The sun was shining and we took a picnic so we could sit by the lake. I took the most amazing photo of Logan as he had held his head up, whilst laid down. He was staring out over the lake and watching the world go by. We all joined him in just watching and feeling some painful peace. Swagger sat with us as well. There were tears, but we tried to just be happy and enjoy the moment. Swagger was also very calm. Maybe he knew, we will never know. But certainly, it was a beautiful hour relaxing in the warm sun on the cold January day. He had some time standing and he took in lots of smells. He was happy.

On the way home I popped into the butchers. I was getting him a goodbye meal. In my head I wanted to get him a big fat juicy steak. As a family, we eat very little meat, but I was not holding back on my boy now. However, the nurse in me stopped me. I couldn't bear the thought of giving him a belly ache for his last few hours. It would be awful to feed him something that didn't agree with him just because I thought that's what we traditionally want to give. I opted for the most expensive six sausages they had. I had to work so hard not to cry. They asked me what flavour do I want? I thought "it doesn't really matter, since they are for the dog". But I didn't say that. I just said the first one that I noticed the label of, and I took my sausages and left. I have never been back to that butchers since and I'm not sure I ever will. That said, I do have other dogs and I will probably go and get their goodbye meal there too, so we shall see.

I took the sausages home and we carried on with our day, like it was any other day. This was so hard to do, but we had to still function. On all possible occasions, we were cuddling our boy. He laid on our laps enjoying mummy and daddy time. Paige was there, also getting in on the cuddles.

Thursday

Thursday arrived, another day, like any other. But to us, also only one day left. Brian and I spoke again and again. "Are you happy and at peace with the decision?" "Are you sure it's the right time?" The answer was always "yes" and "yes". As painful as it was, it was yes. We were also just happy that we had this peaceful time to say goodbye and that he had not further deteriorated, so we were safe to wait. He still had a sparkle in his eye and we were keen that he didn't lose that. Paige went to school, we had to work, but Logan got all his cuddles as we tag teamed his care. We were so lucky to be able to do this.

We also took the time to tell Paige the plan. She was ok. We recognised that she will have been processing it all and probably not really understanding the gravity of what was to come. We did what we felt was best. She understood. She was sad but not in tears. She just understood the end was coming. We also asked if she still wanted to go to the party. She was adamant that she did, so we left the plan in place, for our friend to relay her there and back and stay to make sure she was ok.

I still saw my patients and clients this day, but I also asked my admin assistant to call my clients for the next day and cancel them. She did this with complete care. I was so grateful to have her handle all of this. I was not ready for her to cancel my work for next week, as that would mean the deed was done. I was not going to commit to that until it was actually done. She understood this completely and handled the coming days with nothing more than the odd text from me.

Friday

Friday: the hideous day had arrived. Paige went off to school. My mission for the day was to prepare the house and make it all about Logan. I got him up and took him out for his walk in the buggy. We only went to the usual park. He knew this place well. I decided to take cutters so that I could cut foliage and all sorts of other items from the park areas he usually sniffed at. I'm not totally sure if I did this due to some weird sixth sense that it was the right thing to do, or whether I had just absorbed enough of my elderly patient care that I had preached for so long, that it was just second nature. Either way, I wanted him to be surrounded by all the things he knew and loved. These smells were the smells of his local social network. They were his Facebook, his Instagram. I put them in his buggy and we slowly meandered around with Swagger running around as well.

It was another beautiful day, with the sun shining again. More photos needed to be taken of the handsome man, watching the world go by. He had some time out of the buggy and stood for a while before I laid him down to relax on the grass for a bit. We finally went home.

Now it was time to cook his sausages. They were prepared with love and slowly given to him through the day when cool. He woofed them down (excuse the pun). We made sure we all gave him two sausages each and Paige gave him her two when she got home from school.

I prepared the space. This had to be perfect. Covid was still a bad smell in the air so technically home visits were still supposed to happen outside. But it was January. Most weather is ok to work around but the rain is not. My boy loved the outside so I actually did want it done in the garden, but the light would also have been poor as it was winter.

I took a lot of care over his area. I knew the vet would be arriving in an hour, so I had to be ready. I laid his car travel bed in front of the patio doors. That way there was shelter but we were practically outside anyway. I laid all the foliage I had picked earlier, around the bed. I also put essential oils on the bed. Vanilla, coconut, valerian and ginger. These are scientifically proven to be the most calming smells for dogs, so they were going down. For good measure I also sprayed Pet Remedy and Adaptil. In for a penny in for a pound, I was not missing any angle. His senses will be happy. Finally, I dimmed the lights, only as much as I could so the vet could still see. I turned on calming music. I know that science says dogs are most calmed by reggae music, but that was never going to be appropriate, and I needed to think of us too. So calming relaxation music was played. The scene was set and now we had to wait.

We also kept speaking to Paige. She had decided she did want to be present to say goodbye and be with him. She also very much wanted to be with me. We also encouraged our other dog to be present too. He was a little more stressed by it all, so he tucked himself into a corner and we did not force him to come any closer. This was fine. He could have chosen to leave completely but he didn't.

The vet arrived with her nurse and although she was an hour late, that didn't matter at all, it meant we had an extra hour with our boy.

The vet was kind and spoke to us in all the ways we needed to be spoken to. I remember very little of what actually happened now, but I do remember some nuggets. I remember that the nurse who was there to assist, actually disappeared. I spoke to her weeks after the event, and she told me that she went because she too was crying. Our efforts had moved her. It really is an act that gets into the stomach of every veterinary professional. We know we are doing a kindness, but that doesn't mean it doesn't hurt too. Even when we have never met the fur baby, it still hits us.

The vet went to place the cannular and I held my boy. I cried and cried. I had to wear a mask due to Covid. We all did. By now my mask was nothing more than a soaking wet snot holder. I had to take it off when it got too full. Everyone understood, it was inevitable. Logan sparked our hearts though. He was Logan right until the end. When the vet leaned in to touch his leg, he did his famous air snap. He always did it to the vets. "Let them know who's boss" he would say. But he knew I was boss really, so he only ever did one air snap. I had him and cuddled him, and it was all good. The vet did ask if I wanted to muzzle him though. "No" was all I could get out. Not a chance in the world!

There is only one thing I do regret of my goodbye. I had got wet cotton wool ready to prepare his leg. I had also done his shave so that all those things did not need doing by the vet. It was all with me. But the nurse had got out a swab with Hibiscrub on it. The vet then used this. I do wish I had the strength to say my piece. For many of my professional goodbyes, I have never used any clinical smelling swabs and neither had my vets. There was no need. Yes, the leg needed to be wet, but it didn't need to be sterile and clean. We are saying goodbye. There is no mind changing after that injection is given, so there was no need for that swab. I didn't have the strength to speak. I just let it happen. I knew at the time, but I let it happen. There was nothing actually wrong with this, so I let it be. It wasn't the time to argue. Thankfully I had done so much else, that I doubt it really mattered to my boy. He had spent a lifetime of me taking him into vets with me for work and me cleaning his cuts and scrapes with the Hibiscrub, so it wasn't really that unfamiliar. I do just wish I had said something at the beginning so that they knew my wish there. No matter though, I had a whole heap of wins for this moment, and I rejoice in that.

My Paige sat on Brian's knee. Brian sat stroking Logan's back end. I sat cradling my boy. The vet let the injection flow and our boy quickly and peacefully drifted off to sleep. There could not be a more peaceful goodbye. No more perfect goodbye. It was done. He was gone.

The moment that followed is something I will never forget. It started to snow. Logan loved the snow. He loved running in it and biting at it. When we made snowmen, he would dig at the bottom of them and make them fall over. We used to throw loose snowballs at him, and he would catch and bite them. This was incredible. It snowed for only a few minutes, but it snowed hard for that few minutes. We knew this was Logan's spirit being taken to his next home. The one where he will sit watching over us.

The vets left swiftly having given us as much pleasantry as was appropriate in a desperately sad moment.

I wept and wailed. Tears streaming down my face. Brian sobbed.

We were broken. Swagger stayed out of the way, that was his way of coping. Paige cried too. A more peaceful cry. She was not crying like the wailing tantrum children are very capable of. She just shed quiet tears whilst she tried to take it all in. She told us she loved us. She hugged us both hard. We all told each other we loved each other and told Logan we loved him too. He was already up in the stars, but desperately watching over us. I know he will have been trying to hug me like he always did, his head over my neck.

The pain felt was indescribable. Unimaginable. A pain so bad you wonder why you ever did it to yourself. Why get a fur child when this is the end result. I hurt. My body physically hurt. I ached. My face ached. My jaw ached. My chest hurt. My stomach hurt. I had to stop this pain somehow. What could I do? Oh the pain. I can never forget that pain. I know now that it does ease and does hurt less, but you can't see how that is ever possible at that moment.

Paige had stopped crying her little tears and was quiet. It was clear she didn't know what to do with herself. None of us did. There was a knock at the door and it was our friend here to see if Paige wanted to go to the party? She said yes. We didn't hold a long conversation. We asked her and she was sure, so she went. Our friend knew that the slightest sign of an issue and she was to circle back. Paige was already changing her focus. She was actually lucky. She now didn't have to feel any pain. Children live in the moment. Right now, her moment was party time. Good for her to be free of the pain.

I needed this space too. I now didn't have to worry about how she felt. I now had support from someone else I trusted, to help me for those two hours. This was so kind. But now I was back stuck in my pain and so was Brian.

We needed a distraction. We couldn't cope. We needed to calm down and rest somehow. This was when the foliage I had picked came into its own. I don't know how I thought of it. Desperation might have made my brain think of anything and in that moment it came up with the most beautiful idea.

Logan's Wreath I made from the items that surrounded his bed in his final moments

I picked up all the foliage from around Logan, who was laid peacefully on his bed, and I decided to make it into a bouquet. I got out the hot glue gun and I glued a few tennis balls in place too. It was a beautiful and fitting tribute. Brian was also struggling. I found some small wooden signs. They were from a fairy garden Paige had been given. Now they would be tribute signs for Logan's bouquet. Brian wrote beautiful words on the signs and I stuck them in the bouquet. I placed the bouquet on his chest. I know I thought a lot about covering him over, but I didn't. It felt too final. I felt like if I covered him over, when I uncover him, he might actually look dead. Right now, he just looked like Logan. I didn't want him to look different. I don't even know why I felt like this. I have seen enough passed fur babies to know they don't actually look any different. But you can tell their spirit has left them. I don't know how, but you can tell.

Paige was soon back from her party. We had composed ourselves a little by then. She had had a great time. She had spoken to her friends about it, and they were very supportive, but not saddened by what she had told them. Our friend had kept a very close eye on her and felt confident she had not wanted to come back. She had even sent me a text halfway through the party to reassure us that all was well. I was also glad she had gone as it meant she had eaten as food was the last thing on our minds.

Paige made her own memorials out of bits of ribbon, as children do. She wrote him messages and we got her to bed. It had been a very long day, and we were sure sleep was needed.

We needed sleep too. We needed it but it didn't happen. I know we did manage to stop the tears for short periods of time, but everything sparked us off again. The food bowl, the lead, the beds all over the house. The toys that were his favourites. So many things.

We encouraged Swagger to walk around Logan in the hope that it might help him with his grief. We are not sure how bothered he was. He didn't seem to be at the time. We just know we did what we could to help him understand that Logan was gone. I suspect he was actually more distressed by the anguish we were clearly feeling.

The next morning

Our first day without Logan was a tough day. By now, all days were tough, but a new kind of tough each time. Each new challenge was hard all over again. We got up early in the morning. We had eventually cried ourselves to sleep. We had slept, but more of that passed out type of sleep. Not the type where you have drifted off comfortably.

We woke up with the puffiest of eyes, barely able to open them. One of my eyes was slightly less swollen on one edge. It was really noticeable for me as it felt so odd. I guess it was from the pressure of the pillow, as I had laid on that side. I went straight down to see my boy. I was, of course, scared of what he might look like. That worry that he might now look different was in my mind. I had to get there before Paige, and make sure he was dignified and as handsome as always. I opened the door. He looked just like Logan. I had no need to worry.

He had needed some cleaning. His bowel had now relaxed and you could see his tail a little raised, it was the only part that was perhaps a little sad, as it did not look like him. I cleaned him up and that was that. I was happy to keep him clean. It didn't take much effort at all and was one of the last things I was able to do for him.

I stroked him again and knelt at his side sobbing. He was now not quite feeling like my boy. He was cold and his skin felt hard. His fur was still so soft, but rigor mortis had set in. His limbs didn't move.

He had most definitely gone. But there was a comfort in knowing that he has most definitely gone, as it was his funeral next.

We went to get dressed for the event. There was a funny moment, a slight reprieve from the sadness. I chucked on my walking clothes. That felt right. It's what we did as a family, and it was a happy place for us all. I turned around to look at my husband just in time to see him sliding his arms into his black suit jacket, that he has reserved for human funerals. I looked at him in silence and he said "well, one of us has missed the mark!" We both laughed. It felt like the first smile we had had for days. I explained my choice and he very quickly agreed and changed.

It was odd. I felt guilt for that moment of laughter. It felt wrong, even though it was so well needed. I know now that Logan wouldn't want me to never laugh again, but at the time, smiles came with a wallop of guilt soon after.

We went downstairs and I finally covered him up. Up until now I had not wanted to cover him up. I still had that fear that if I covered him, he might change how he looked and then I would be scared when I uncovered him. But the time had come to take him outside and into the car, so now there was no choice. Our boy's passing was private. We had told our neighbours, mostly so that they understood why we might be upset and not speak to them outside, but we didn't want them seeing our boy now.

Silently we all got in the car and drove to the crematorium, Dignity, so correctly named.

The crematorium

We arrived. We had not been here before, so we had to figure out our way around the place. Thankfully the staff were wonderful. They had been amazing on the phone and now were amazing in person. I was struggling to speak. My husband asked what to do. They directed us to pull the car up to a certain spot. This meant it was private for us and we could move Logan onto a trolley. I was so nervous of leaving him at any point. I had no reason to be worried though. We lifted him onto the new trolley where they had fresh incontinence sheets for him to lie on. They then wheeled him to the farewell room where we were directed to go. Brian moved the car and then we all went to the room where Logan was waiting for us. They had put him in there to allow us to have some time with him.

This time was for us to think, reflect and say our goodbyes. There were some formalities that of course, you would rather not have to deal with, but you can't get away from formalities these days. We were also encouraged to think about what type of urn we may want and if we wanted any type of memorial. There was also information on bereavement help. We felt very cared for.

We didn't do any memorials at this point. We did have a good look at all the options, just in case, but we had a firm plan and we were happy with this. I had an urn that I had been gifted by my great aunt when she died. It was old and a very random gift, but it was so suitable. I asked for the crematorium to put him in this and they were very happy to oblige. It saved us money, but more importantly, there was a family connection to his final resting place. We handed over the white and blue urn, and they left with it.

We also didn't do any memorials, as I had done so many already. I had a lifetime of memories, and I wanted his memorials to be made before he died, not after; that way they didn't need to feel sad. I had paw prints and a tree hanging ornament. I was all good for memories. I didn't opt to keep any fur. I was worried about what it might feel like if I actually lost that fur later on. I did have plans for some of his ashes though. Sadly, that would clearly have to wait. I was not ready to organise that yet. I needed to get this step out of the way first.

The funeral

It was time. After about twenty minutes, a staff member came in to see if we were ready. There was no point in waiting. It was odd; you don't want the moment to end as you don't want him gone, but he was already gone, so, then you want it over with. My mind was a roller coaster of emotion. That is the best description.

As we had an attended funeral, it was our privilege to wheel his trolley to the chamber. We had said our goodbyes. We had kissed his cold, soft head, we had laid his wreath on him and now we were taking him to the last part of his earthly shell's journey.

We sobbed again.

When we arrived at the cremation chamber the staff was desperately kind and compassionate. They explained about certain things which meant we had more decisions to make. They showed us the empty chamber to assure us of how clean it was and that it will only be our boy in there and therefore, only his ashes that will come back to us. It was both awkward and reassuring at the same time. They kindly allowed for his wreath to go in with him. That made us so happy as this was made up of the smells and messages from his walks and a few of his beloved balls.

They did explain that this would mean there were factors that we may not want to see and that it may be better to not actually see him go into the cremation chamber. We certainly agreed. Just like a human cremation, you would never see that part, you would simply see the departure of the coffin.

We stepped back to a marked zone that meant we would not see anything that we later could not unsee. This was good for us all. Paige was with us too and at all the parts of this journey we had asked if she wanted to be with us and join in, and she always did.

Once we had stood back the staff member stood beautifully and respectfully with a bowed head. He spoke a few words that brought us all to tears again. I do wish I could remember what he said. I promised myself I would never forget, but I was too emotional. The words have gone. All I know is that this was perfect and beautiful. It felt like a small prayer, whilst not being religious at all. It felt like these complete strangers actually cared for my boy as well. I had not expected that. They said they do this for all their goodbyes.

It's well worth sharing at this point, that I bumped into the owner of this crematorium about six months later at a veterinary conference. I thanked him for the incredible service, and I desperately held back my tears as I was trying to be professional, whilst saying something so personal. He told me that they also have spiritual healers come monthly to help any spirits move on, that might be stuck in the area. It was so beautiful to hear. Whatever your views are on the afterlife and spirits, it was warm and uplifting, to hear the efforts they go to, to ensure every view and every possibility is thought of and addressed. I couldn't have been happier to hear him say that, and from what I saw, I can believe they would move the world if it would make the goodbye any better.

It was done. Logan was gone. We had been by his side for the whole goodbye. We now had to let go. We repeated our goodbyes and told him we loved him again. Certainly, that was not the final time we spoke to him, we still speak to him even now. We just had nothing else to say than to thank the wonderful staff and keep telling Logan we loved him.

We also found ourselves constantly saying "sorry". I know that was silly as we had done nothing but love him and care for him and then give him this, the final gift of a dignified and peaceful goodbye at the perfect time in the perfect surroundings. But somehow, we still felt guilty, like maybe there was something else we could do or have done. With every "sorry", Brian and I reassured each other that we had done the right thing. It's amazing how many times the same conversation can go around in your mind. The whole time our amazing daughter listened and hugged us.

We walked out of the crematorium and got into the car having been told he would be ready for collection in three hours. This was fine. We were not going to risk any delivery going wrong or any time delay. I needed to keep control of anything I could and if that meant three hours of wandering around the local town with our sunglasses on in January, then so be it! Thankfully, it was a sunny day.

Once on our own we had a moment to regroup. We decided to get out of the car and have a walk around the garden of remembrance first. It was nice to take in the area that his spirit might possibly choose to stay in. I didn't believe it would. He was staying with me. But we wanted to have a look around. We desperately needed some fresh air and to drink some water. We were all so dehydrated from all the crying.

The garden was beautiful. It went up the side of a hill. There were so many memorials. Some old, some new, some faded, some fancy. There was a lot of variety. There was also an herb garden. I loved that and took some photos. There were wonderful herbs for dogs, to help them feel calm, or for digestion and such like. They were all labelled and it was very inspiring and comforting to see the extra care that was taken.

We finally went back to the car and decided to head to the local town to park up and walk to fill more time. We were in no fit state to go into the shops really, so we enjoyed the picturesque, chocolate box village by appreciating its beauty. We walked through an orchard and found some fields. It was a slow meander. We spent the time reminiscing on stories of Logan. Paige was wonderful and very happy to fill the time with her stories of him. We knew this was a good thing for her to do.

When we realised that the time had passed surprisingly fast, we headed back, but not before stopping in an old vintage sweet shop, to get Paige some sweets. She most definitely deserved the treat.

When we got back to the crematorium, all the mixed emotions resurfaced again. Scared of what I might see, missing my dear boy that bit more (if that was even possible) happy to have him back even though it was in his new state of ashes, worried that we had not decided what to do with his ashes.

We got out the car and went to the office. They were wonderful again. We sobbed again. They left us to wait in a special room so that we had privacy before they brought him through in a brown paper gift bag. Inside was his urn and in there, his ashes. They gave us a card as well. It was such kindness. We didn't look inside the bag or urn. That was to be done in the privacy of home, with our cup of tea, as us English always do. Tea for every occasion. This was definitely a moment for tea.

We quietly and gratefully thanked the staff and left for our quiet drive home.

Back at home

The tears were now starting to slow down. But this meant the guilt kicked in. Why was I not crying? Does that make me a bad person? Do I not miss him anymore? Don't I love him? The answer is no. You just can't cry like that one hundred percent of the day. It's just not possible. There were still plenty of tears and pain, I just was able to have some peace too. I really needed the peace because my tummy and thigh muscles were aching so much. My face hurt. It was crazy. I hadn't realised how much effort you use when you cry! Madness!

Logan in his urn

Brian made us tea. Our next job was to open the urn. We just wanted to see what he now looked like and make sure he was in there. It was very heavy, but we had to be sure. I lifted the lid off the urn and inside was a small, dried-flower posy. That was me crying again at this little touch of magic and care. Was there no end to this care? Under the black tissue paper were his ashes. This was not actually something I had ever seen before. Logan's dust. The physical mark he left on the planet. It was white and had various sized particles. I didn't touch it. I was not going to risk losing any. He was staying in his new bed. We replaced the lid and popped him back down.

We had not made any decision on what to do with the ashes. I had by now decided that I wanted to get a memorial that did incorporate his ashes, but I had to take time to think about this as it was a big commitment and I was scared in case anything went wrong with that process. This was not a decision for today.

Logan sat in his urn for a number of weeks moving around. He actually moved around the house as we found ourselves picking him up, having a chat, giving the urn a stroke and popping him down again where we were. I know that was risky. What if we dropped him? But we never did the whole time he was alive, so why would we now? This was what we needed. I even came home one day to find Brian sat on the sofa, watching the television with Logan sat next to him under his arm. Some might laugh at that, but I thought it was wonderful. He knew what he needed and even now, Logan could provide it. Brian also took comfort in writing a diary. He would regularly stop and write his memories of Logan down. This might be at any time and on any random piece of paper. His biggest fear was forgetting our boy. That paper still sits in his bedside table to this day.

Paige quite quickly started making pocket Logans that afternoon. She called them this. She is a crafter and always has been so seeing her sat making things was not unusual. She sat with her scissors and pencils, then came in and showed us her Logan she had drawn and cut out. He was lovely and we praised her of course. On that, she popped him in her pocket and carried on with her day. We know this was her coping strategy and it was very healthy, so we were thrilled she had found a way so fast.

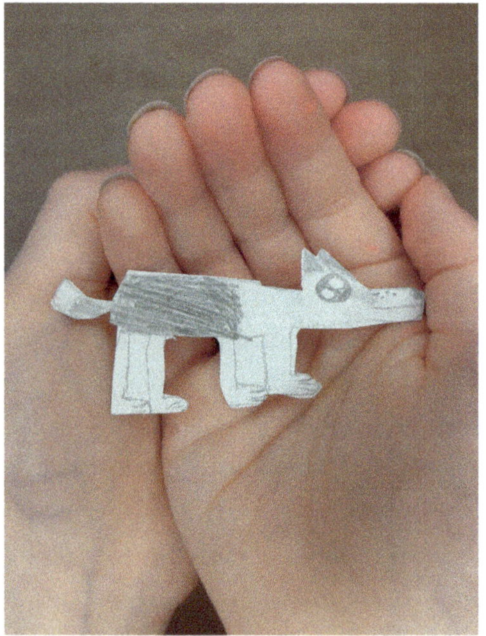

Pocket Logan, by Paige

Pocket Logans became a regular thing. She often made them at school too so now she had her boy wherever she was. The teacher told us how much she talked about him. Clearly, we were very lucky she was such an open child. Her pocket Logans remain a common thing even to this day, as does her love of talking about him. She even makes pocket Logans for her friends, and her teaching assistant recently told us that they have a game where every day they make a sentence where they have to include a word of the day. Paige will always find a sentence where she can also add "Logan", and the teaching assistant does the same always using the word "Madonna". I am proud that his energy lives on and still puts a smile on, not only my daughter's face, but also those around her.

Swagger

We had several people say to us "oh well, at least you have another dog". This statement was not particularly comforting. It's not like Swagger was a spare. They are completely different beings. But I do understand that under pressure, when trying to find words of comfort this type of sentence can be the first thing that comes to mind.

Having a second dog was indeed a blessing, but it was also a double-edged sword.

It did help that we had Swagger, of course, but he was not quite as family orientated as Logan was, so we didn't want to pressure him into being our comfort blanket if he didn't want to be. We had cuddles when he chose to give them to us, but we could not, and would not, force him. Logan was the type of dog who would be at your side with his head over your leg, arm or neck when you were crying. Swagger in the same position would choose to hide in the corner and hope no one saw him until the pressure had passed, then he would come out, assess the situation and decide if he wanted to give you a cuddle. They were very different personalities.

Alongside this, we were grieving about all the aspects we no longer had with Logan, but yet having to still do them. Feeding only Swagger. The ritual of picking up two empty bowls, was now only one. Getting food out of only one of the food tubs and not the other.

It's quite amazing what you notice. Even doing the poop pick, in the garden, you know which poop was Logan's and which was Swagger's. It brought tears to our eyes to know we were picking up the last of his poops!

There was also the guilt of having time back. We had not really realised how time consuming it was looking after Logan. We were full time careers. Now we didn't need to keep scooping him up when he had a poo tail. We didn't need to keep giving him cuddles because he had asked for a cuddle. We didn't need to sort out his medicines and all the supplements I had added to the diet to keep him with happy guts. No more washing of incontinence sheets. No more putting him in the stair lift to go to bed and to get him up in the morning. No more warm baths. No more walking him around the garden balancing him and now the guilt of feeling a little relieved that I wouldn't have a sore back with that challenge again. There was an endless list of things we missed but still had to do with Swagger, which most definitely caused conflict in the mind.

We loved Swagger dearly so there was no issue there, but it was so hard to do everything for one dog and not two.

It was really hard to get out on the first dog walk without Logan. That was one of the toughest things I have ever had to do. We couldn't bring ourselves to do it for a few days. We went for the first time on the Monday. I had to psych myself up as I knew it would be hard picking only one lead off the hook. Logan's lead was still there and actually, it still is to this day. As soon as I picked up that lead, I started to cry. Paige was at school so that was one less issue. Brian was home so there was good support.

We left the house much faster than before, because I didn't have to put on boots that protected Logan's toes as they dragged a little when he walked. I didn't have to get out the buggy, this was now redundant. We set off with Swagger who was super happy to be on his walk, but Brian and I were trying to hold back the tears. It was pointless trying really.

Thankfully on that first walk we didn't bump into anyone we knew. This helped as we were not ready to talk about it with near strangers. This did happen on many occasions that followed. "Oh, don't I usually see you with two dogs?" "Yes, you do, but sadly I've lost Logan. He was old and it was time" I'd reply. It was often awkward, but we would get through the small talk and pleasantries and finish the walk.

The people

Over the coming weeks we had a constant stream of support from so many people. It was really quite amazing and so touching, that most of the support came from the fellow dog lovers of the world, and my clients, rather than friends and family.

My friends and family of course were lovely, but I think on reflection, not that many of them had been through the type of care level created by a high dependency dog. Most of my clients had high dependency dogs, that was why they were seeing me. So, they just understood.

It is fair to say some people really are amazing in a crisis and just know how to offer support. I don't know how these people learn to be this way, but I am grateful that they are. I guess it might be sad to think too hard about how they may have learnt to be a rock for others.

One friend dropped round a gift bag on the night we had said goodbye to Logan. She did not knock or disturb us. She left the bag on the doorstep and sent a message so we knew to look. She must have heard via Paige at the party. She dropped round what I call a survival bag. In it was an assortment of items. Pot noodles, so we had super easy food to eat (we did eat those that night as we knew we had to eat something; they oddly worked), chocolate, lavender bubble bath, a book for Paige, and many more items for all of us and

Paige. It was so kind and so needed.

When we came down the day after Logan had gone, that painful yet sunny morning, we noticed nothing. But when we did have to step outside and open the front door, there was the most beautiful bouquet of red roses. One of my clients had driven over and left them at the door. It was such kindness. We kept one of the roses and dried it out and have it to this day sitting with his silhouette.

Later that day there was a gift of a Loganberry bush on the front doorstep. We all cried again. Loganberry; how perfect. Now we needed to get a giant pot and make this memorial pot for my boy. We were so touched. This client, and many more of them, were really now friends and she had been so supportive in my discussions in the last few weeks so she knew the journey I was on. She often cried with me. She had decided on this Loganberry bush long ago and had ordered when she knew Logan's time was short. This year, we actually had our first harvest of Loganberries that was enough to make jam. It was the most beautiful jam we have ever made. Just perfect. It is wonderful to have him in our lives in this way.

Over the weeks the gifts poured in. The generosity was huge and we felt so loved and supported. We had forget-me-not seeds, key rings, chocolates and flowers. So many cards that I still have today. Some more gifts continued to make me cry. I got a necklace which I had never seen before. It was a projection necklace that you held up to the light and you could see my boys face right there! If you shone a light through it, you could project him onto the wall. I did this a lot. The photo was perfect. He was in his buggy, looking right at me with his tongue poking out. It so often was poking out. We always joked about his giant tongue that was far too big for his head!

We had a gift arrive a few months later. It was little wonder it took so long. It was a beautiful clay model of my boy. It was a perfect likeness and brought a lump to my throat. More mixed emotion. By now, thoughts of him were starting to make me smile again rather than cry. Was this acceptable? Of course it was, but at the time you worry that you are not doing justice to the memory of your loved one. That model continues to take pride of place in the family space, right where he belongs.

Logan today

Sometimes we think that maybe we should put his ashes in the Loganberry pot. But I worry that the pot will break in a frost or the bush will die. In the end, we always decide to just leave him where he is.

He sits in the window. The window he loved to look out of when he was watching the street go by. He sits there, with a few of the keyrings we were sent as gifts and his collar. We still lean over the sofa and pat the lid of his urn and wish him a good night when we pop the blind down. I have concluded that he will probably go wherever I go when it's my turn to meet my maker. So, until then, our home will be his home. Our whole family are all in full support of this.

It is unnerving to think that my boy has been gone two years now. I feel shocked that all this time has passed, and he can still bring a tear to our eyes. My daughter still makes pocket Logans. Two years on and I still have this all so fresh in my mind. Two years on and I feel the need to write this all down. Two years on and the trauma is still so raw.

I decided to write this book in the hope that it can help even one person. I know that I am not the only one to tread this path and feel this pain. I know I am not the only one to feel the love this strong for their fur baby so many years later. I know the love for my boy will never go. He will be here forever. I want to share this so that others can know, this is normal. This is ok. This is love.

A short note

After I had finished writing this memoir, I contacted Dignity to speak to the owner and share that I had written this book. He kindly offered to read it. His reaction to the book was highly complimentary, and most importantly, he shared this note:

"The committal we said was "God Bless you Logan, May your Spirit Go In Peace and Go Towards The Light" – we say this for every pet."

Thank you for sharing these kind words with me again. They still bring a lump to my throat, but it's a warmth at the same time.

Preparation ideas list

Here I have prepared a list of the things I had to think about in preparation of the best goodbye I could possibly give my boy. My final gift to him. It is not an exhaustive list as everyone will have thought of other things. It won't even be a complete list of all the things you have to do, as everyone is different.

This is just a list that might help, and I really hope that it does.

1. Emergency vets phone number and address in your phone. If you go on holiday make sure you find out this information for the local area.

2. Ring your vets to find out what services they offer so you feel prepared. If it's not what you require, ring around and find one that will offer what you want.

3. Consider using an internet search to see if there are specific home euthanasia service providers in your area, as this is a growing service and I am sure it will only get better.

4. Book your cremation or other type of service you may want. If you want to bury your loved one somewhere other than a registered pet burial ground, find out any local rules and pick your spot. Be well prepared and happy with your choices. Have your plan ready.

5. It's worth thinking about any urn or memorial you might like to have before the event. This takes pressure off deciding later and will help you to not feel like you should have done something else.

6. Choose if there are any final activities or meals you might like to do in your last few days, or hours.

7. Decide how you might like to set the scene of the final moment. What would your fur baby like to have around them. What smells and sounds. Any toys or loved items? What bedding?

8. Incontinence sheets and wipes (or any other cleaning items you might like; you may want gloves). These are needed for underneath them and to clean them up as they are likely to release their bladder and bowel in time.

9. Have your questions or requests written down to give to the vet in case you are unable to think of them when they arrive.

10. Decide if you need any other friends and family to support you. You may not know how much support you need, so it might be worth reaching out to a friend to prepare them, in case you need them.

11. Tell your neighbours if you know the date and approximate time in advance, so that you don't have to worry if you don't feel like talking when the time comes.

12. If you have any other fur children or skin children, make appropriate plans for them and help them through their grief. This will vary. There is no right answer, but you may want to do some research to help you feel prepared and have a plan.

13. Have the phone number of a bereavement councillor in case you need it. There is no shame in this, and some charities, such as the Blue Cross (in the UK) offer this service specifically for the grief of losing fur babies.

14. Have lots of water available and ensure you remember to drink it. You do need to try to look after yourself now too.

You have been the carer for someone else. Now it's time for you. Lip balm and face moisturiser is also a good idea as you will get so dehydrated and uncomfortable from all the tears.

15. Have some easy food available. You may well not want to eat, and you are unlikely to want to cook. So, anything that is quick and easy is more likely to be useful to get nutrition of some sort into your body. You can't eat like that for long, but it's very helpful in the early stages of your grief.

16. Vases. I wouldn't suggest you need lots on tap, but it's worth asking a neighbour if you might be able to borrow some, should you be inundated with love.

17. Give yourself time. Let yourself grieve. This might well mean time off work so keep your workplace informed and hopefully they will be kind and understanding.

Bereavement support

The Pet Loss Support Help line:
https://www.bluecross.org.uk/about-pet-loss-support
0800 096 6606 (UK)

The Ralph Site: https://www.theralphsite.com/

Please know there are different methods for bereavement support. There is no shame in reaching out for help. You may need a skilled listener, or someone with further qualifications who can offer coping methods. It is completely normal to need more support and guidance on your grief journey. You can search online to find the right person that fits your needs. They can give you the correct support for your individual journey. "Pet grief counsellor" can be a useful online search term.

There are many wonderful resources by way of websites and books, that can help you.

Cremation Support and further information for planning
Association of Private pet cemeteries and crematoria:
https://appcc.org.uk/

Pet cremation services: https://www.petcremationservices.co.uk/